AN ANTHOLOGY OF POETRY
BEARERS OF BLACKNESS

Hazel Clayton Harrison, editor

Ginny Knight, artist

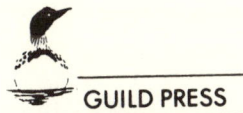

GUILD PRESS
P.O. Box 22583
Robbinsdale, MN.
55422

BEARERS OF BLACKNESS
was made possible in part
by assistance from
Larson Publications, Osseo, Minnesota

BEARERS OF BLACKNESS
was prepared for publication at
Guild Press West
P.O. Box 3395
Manhattan Beach, CA 90266

Books should be ordered from
Guild Press
P.O. Box 22583
Robbinsdale, MN 55422

International Standard Book Number 0-940248-29-8
Library of Congress Catalog Card Number 86-83352
Copyright © 1987 Guild Press

ALL RIGHTS RESERVED
Reproduction in whole or in part without written permission is prohibited,
except by a reviewer who may quote brief passages in a review
Manufactured in the United States of America
by Barry J. Kiel and Associates, Brooklyn Park, MN

BEARERS OF BLACKNESS

Introduction by Hazel Clayton-Harrison, editor 1

PART ONE: I AM EARTHBOUND 2-11
"Earthbound" by Ken Wibecan 2
"The Color Of My Skin" by Maurice W. Britts 3
"Revival" by Charlene Higginbotham 3
"Suicide Of A Puerto Rican Jibaro" by Alberto O. Cappas 4
"Hardtimes" by Diane E. Sterling 5
"Jamaican Night Watchman" by Maryetta Kelsick Boose 6
"New Chains Holding Me" by Linda Benner-Parker 7
"Southwest Township" by Ginny Knight 7
"Ethiopian Night" by Ken Wibecan 8
"In Dark Eyes" by Bernard V. Finney, Jr. 9
"Photograph of a 1923 Lynching" by Ken Wibecan 10
"Word Usage" by George D. Clabon 11

PART TWO: BRING ME YOUR LOVE 12-18
"No Room In The Inn" by Louis A. Chase 12
"And This Bed Reminds Me" by Cynthia Williams 13
"Flowers" by Leon Knight 14
"Family Reunion" by Hazel Bell 14
"My Best" by Angela Kinamore 15
"Our Last Goodbye" by Sharon C. Terry 16
"Love Poem IX" by Hasani B. Julian 17
"Sharing(?)" by Essie Caldwell Kammin 17
"Powerful Words Of Love" by Beverly A. Russell 18

PART THREE: WE BE QUEENS 19-28
"We Be Queens" by Beverly A. Russell 19
"Poem For Revolutionary Women" by Hazel Clayton Harrison 20
"Secrets Of A Black Woman" by Uilani Enola Jackmon 20
"An Uncommon, Common Woman" by Leon Knight 21
"Mama's Hands" by Pauline Bady 22
"Women Raise Mens" by Angela Kinamore 23
"The Nile Flows North" by Linda Benner-Parker 24
"Aging Lady Of Love" by Maryetta Kelsick Boose 24
"Song Of A Single Mother" by Lorraine Bryant 25
"The 'Stuff' Of Heroes" by Ginny Knight 26
"Night Song" by Shirley Dougan King 27
"Do Me A Favor" by Diane E. Sterling 28

BEARERS OF BLACKNESS

PART FOUR: OUR CHILDREN WILL INHERIT	**29-35**
"Our Children Will Inherit" by Ginny Knight	29
"Prayer For A Black Child" by Mary J. Kyle	30
"Two In One" by Odessa Cleveland	30
"Blind Conscience" by Patricia M. Johnson	31
"Lullabye To A Sweet Brown Baby" by Alcleata Hamilton Williams	32
"Positive Reflections" by Hasani B. Julian	33
"Running, Running, Running" by Rosa Bogar	33
"Wind Chimes (for JoAnn)" by Sandy Macebuh	34
"On The Wings Of Their Hopes" by Hazel Bell	35
"Sing Children Sing" by Odessa Cleveland	35
PART FIVE: MAKE STRONG MEN SING	**36-41**
"Mother Didn't Tell Me To Cry" by Gene A. Williams	36
"For The Men Who Sire Us" by Phyllis J. Sloan	37
"The Crossing" by Leon Knight	38
"Man On The Corner" by Sharon C. Terry	39
"De Waters And De Crys" by Kenya Keita Kenyatta Samuels	40
"Father To Son" by Sidney Singleton Sr.	41
"The Guitar Man" by George D. Clabon	41
PART SIX: SOMETHING HAS AROUSED ME	**42-50**
"Something Has Aroused Me" by Beverly A. Russell	42
"The Black Press" by Arlee Bullard Blakey	43
"Saturday At The Inglewood Farmers' Market" by Hazel Clayton Harrison	44
"Hospitality In LA" by Phyllis J. Sloan	45
"If You Don't Know" by Dennis DeLoach	46
"The Big House On The Hill" by Hazel Clayton Harrison	47
"Immortal Afrikan Spirit" by Jamal Ali	47
"Strong Black Woman" by Phyllis J. Sloan	48
"Ain't Never Gonna Die" by Charlene Higginbotham	48
"Our Black Protectors" by Antonia Apolinario	49
"What's Destined To Come" by Angela Kinamore	50
Notes About The Authors	51-52

BEARERS OF BLACKNESS

INTRODUCTION

When Leon Knight, Senior Editor of Guild Press, asked me to edit *Bearers of Blackness*, I was excited about the idea of an anthology of black poetry by talented authors from all over the country. My only reservation was the title. In my mind, *Bearers of Blackness* conjured up images of poets bearing the burden of passing on black culture to future generations. But Leon, who always seems to look on the bright side of things, pointed out that *bear* not only means to to shoulder responsibility, but it also means to carry or bring. He reminded me that in traditional Africa, the poet had the important function of passing on the cultural essence of the people -- of giving voice to the collective conscience.

Then it dawned on me that *Bearers of Blackness* actually represents both sides of the picture. Like the dark side of the moon, it represents the struggles and pain black people have endured. Like the bright side, it represents the joys of passing on black culture to others.

Bearers of Blackness, therefore, brings you both the positive and the negative, the yin and the yang, the ups and the downs of black culture. For example, Part 1, "I am Earthbound," is full of images of chains, nightmares, and lynchings. On the other hand, Part 6, "Something Has Aroused Me," contains poems that are upbeat, uplifting, and reminiscent of the humor and Negro spirituals that helped carry black folks through slavery and reconstruction. So with pride and humility, we offer *Bearers of Blackness*.

Hazel Clayton Harrison, Editor

PART ONE: I AM EARTHBOUND

EARTHBOUND
by Ken Wibecan

I'm tired of writing about Black

I'd rather write about the outdoors
far from the smog and scurry
of civilization

where on a moonless night
the stars float down
like a giant star-filled tea cup
had been inverted
above my head

where on sunny winter mornings
I can strap on my cross-country skis
and make new tracks
through fresh snow
in the silent woods

I want to dream about kings
queens, castles, fanciful creatures
in colorful worlds
where adventure is everyday

where space ships ply the skies
and wondrous beings
with two heads
tenacles, and several pairs of arms
are my best friends

I want to write poems
that make people laugh
smile, remember
and sometimes cry

or stories
about my old dog, Pepe
and fictional tales
for everyone's children
to enjoy

But it is not yet time to fly
I am earthbound
I am black

THE COLOR OF MY SKIN
by Maurice W. Britts

I cried a tear
      Long ago -
The future seemed so bleak.
My mother said,
      "Cheer up, my child,
The future's yours to make
      Don't let that future
Be the color of your skin."

I think back now
      To those words
And know how right she was.
I re-dedicate myself
To throwing off those shackles.
Still - why can't I forget
      The color of my skin?

REVIVAL
by Charlene Higginbotham

middle america has taken out
my bumps and grinds   my sho' nuf
my little colored girl walk
moves stilted in the late afternoon
Black
      has washed up on my mental
      shore all gray and shadowlike
      across time
from   africa   to america's
      dead sandy beach where
big grandma hands
and tired teacher hands
and new doctor hands all dipped
in the dark waters of heritage cup
a white-washed body trying
desperately   to restore its color
trying desperately to restore
      its color.

I AM EARTHBOUND

SUICIDE OF A PUERTO RICAN JIBARO
by Alberto O. Cappas

They didnt understand
They were all americans now
He would smile sometimes
Thinking about his youth
In puerto rico
Carmen/rosa/teresa/liza
Holding on to dreams
That helped him stay alive
The tropical music that was killed
By the new sound of "salsa"
But they didnt understand
His children didnt understand
A million times his body was raped
By the unfriendly cold
The farm he sacrificed
To pursue the american dream
Trying to buy some dignity
At the unemployment office
Shoveling the snow that invaded
His tropical existence
He would walk up virginia street
and down hudson street
Searching
For some clues of understanding
But
Only
Found
New inventions of nightmares
That wanted to destroy his dreams
The dead dreams
That helped him stay alive
Were too weak
for the american nightmare

They didnt understand
They were all americans now.

HARDTIMES
by Diane E. Sterling

Saw your son the other day
head bowed low,
he looked away

saw him again later that night
clothes were torn
his hair a sight

went over to him -
to see what was wrong
clipped me in the head
then he was gone.

When I came to
my wallet was missing
No money inside - not even a dime,
No big deal - much less a crime.

You know, I know -
He knows
that times are hard,
wallets are empty.
Why bother?

I AM EARTHBOUND

JAMAICAN NIGHT WATCHMAN
by Maryetta Kelsick Boose

Dressed in Khaki shirt and pants
(clothes of a night watchman)
you brought me coffee
there by the pool
    and you stayed

    your mouth moved,
    your eyes shone
and   your voice rose when you spoke:
    "I love my black people!
    I love my country!"
And then you repeated it
like a professor making sure
    his class heard.

I didn't mean to be rude
when I closed my eyes.
I was just wondering
how many Blacks say that
    in my country...

NEW CHAINS HOLDING ME
by Linda Benner-Parker

I feel the weight
    of my ancestors' chains
    Each link
--   without rust, without decay
has survived   decades.
    Now
new chains shackle
    my ankles
      squeeze my neck
to near suffocation --
chains built of
    crack, illiteracy
      unemployment, poverty
      teenage pregnancy -
new chains holding me.

SOUTHWEST TOWNSHIP
by Ginny Knight

the sunset over Soweto
    is beautiful
(like sunsets everywhere)
.... but more dies here
    than the day --
hope lies beside
    the future
crumpled in rubble
    mirroring
the too-short sunset
in a river
    of blood.

I AM EARTHBOUND

ETHIOPIAN NIGHT
by Ken Wibecan

slender stick figure
scratches aimlessly
in dried-up memories
of his fertile youth
dust rises in gentle plumes
swiftly disperses
in the frigid evening air

tall shrouded form
glides strongly
through the night
randomly dispensing peace
in the huddled stillness
presents
for the victims

planet turns beckons
the time has come
to change the channel
trading truth for lies
for comfort
they give no Emmys
for reality

IN DARK EYES
by Bernard V. Finney, Jr.

The South African Army, dressed in battle fatigue, waits in the stillness before daybreak. The soldiers, still wet from yesterday's bloody massacre, charge into the township of Soweto. Explosives blow out windows: a bayonet cuts off a mother's breast while she is nursing her newly-born; hard steel clubs crack skulls and maim dreams, and bullets hit the moving shadows that fall in slow motion between the spaces in existence.

The church doors are kicked in and the chalice and Holy Wine are thrown against the wall; prayers are choked by strong hands and tear gas; the Anglican Priest and parishioners are dragged into the streets. God remains at the altar.

This land, blessed by the Sun, is pregnant with diamonds and gold in its womb, but Blacks are not allowed to share in its richness. There is plenty, but the seasons are impotent and the trees are barren for Blacks. Their lives are separate from the totality. The famine and revolution are infinitesimal ticks in dark eyes.

How long must their tables be empty? How long shall Apartheid, dressed in white linen, walk through this land protected by economic and military might?

    The birds, gathering in trees,
            have stopped singing.
    The ticks grow infected
    in dark eyes.

I AM EARTHBOUND

PHOTOGRAPH OF A 1923 LYNCHING
by Ken Wibecan

Fly covered black body
dangling from tree
while long shadow fingers
of evening sun entertain
with bloody light shows

Grotesque darky/scarecrow
fruit of white love
life plucked from him
by goodcitizens
anonymous in their
converted bed sheets.

Wives and children
look on, observe, enjoy it.
Picnic lunches almost gone.
Drinking wine, lemonade, mint juleps
while happy smiles
flush their fishbelly redneck faces

"Shake the tree again, Daddy,
I want to see him dance."

Things were simple then,
one nigger equaled one picnic.
But technology has
advanced with time.
White folks
are more sophisticated now
...and bed sheets come in colors.

WORD USAGE
by George D. Clabon

in conveying the message
in my management team
i use conversational language
that is comfortable to me
as i use words
like can't/won't
    shouldn't
for terms such as
not allowed/against the rules
    prohibited
and find that new labels
are created for me
such as inflexible/blunt
    uncooperative
which makes our discussions
become guarded/protected
    ended
and i return to my desk
pissed/frustrated
    disturbed
that we are creating images
for word usage
that some do not wish used
and the obstacles/barriers
    defenses
they develop
help bring disillusionment
to the dream
as i reach deep inside
for the courage/strength
    motivation
to continue the struggle
for bringing about
understanding language
that is printed/typed
    spoken
in the work environment.

PART TWO: BRING ME YOUR LOVE

NO ROOM IN THE INN
(Christmas - present/future)
by Louis A. Chase

send me no christmas cards
of   mary and joseph
          and the new christ child

cross-over-border people live
          in colexico cages/
the poor
          on the streets/
native americans
          in reservation camps
so,   send me nothing

bring me your love
         silken touches
         strong embraces
         tender kisses
         open spaces
peace to me/   earth
         everyday
let me not
        (like christmas)
             pass away

BEARERS OF BLACKNESS

AND THIS BED REMINDS ME...
by Cynthia Williams

At night I lie awake and remember
    when I would lay beside you
    awake, very awake
I try to find that spot in the bed
    where you used to lay
try to remember how it used to feel
    when you held me tight
    loved me right
And this bed reminds me   of you.

I also have memories of this bed
    wherein I lay in labor
    waiting for the birth
    of my only daughter
I nursed her
    and cradled her in my arms
    while we both dozed
And this bed reminds me   of her.

Yet and still, I lie awake...
    pondering on the world
    wondering why
    so many years have passed by
and I still lie awake...
And this bed reminds me   of them.

BRING ME YOUR LOVE

FLOWERS
(from a patient man)
by Leon Knight

If he returns,
place chrysanthemums
in your window
and test the wetness
of the potting soil each day.
Whenever flowers bloom,
pinch half off and drop them down
where I can reach them,
so I can anoint
the loving places where we lay.

When he leaves again
(as you know he will),
replace the mums with roses
    --half-open buds, just two --
and before those roses fade,
I'll make you forget
why chrysanthemums
meant anything to you.

FAMILY REUNION
(To the Boyers)
by Hazel Bell

We gather together to re-affirm our roots
The familiar stories, we recite in unison
Passing our heritage on to the next one in line
Honoring and remembering my grandfather
And the seeds of hope he planted
I smile, knowing our children will continue
The journey we started.

MY BEST
by Angela Kinamore

I am at my best
when I have you
    beside me.
When I am in your arms,
    feeling safe,
you make me tingle
        inside.

All I care for
is your happiness
    (and you are mine)
and that's what pleases me.

I am at my best
when we are together
    in harmony.
You make my spirit live
    and I dive
straight into myself
    and give
my very best   to you.

OUR LAST GOODBYE
by Sharon C. Terry

Please hurry, go away
Something's in my eye
        I'm cool!
        I'm bold
        I'm brave!
        I'm strong
I really do try
But please hurry
Go away
Something's in my eye

Love was to be forever --
to the very end with you
But   it's over
        oh why
        oh why

Please hurry, go away
Something's in my eye
        I'm cool!
        I'm bold
        I'm brave!
        I'm strong
I really do try
Please, please hurry
    Go away
Something's in my eye...

LOVE POEM IX
by Hasani B. Julian

If you should think of nothing else
I ask you to think of me,
Even to sigh or reprimand
My extreme absurdity.

It's only fair to reciprocate
My often thoughts of you --
As borrower to banker
Forgets not interest due.

SHARING (?)
by Essie Caldwell Kammin

I tried to bring
     me
(a part of Black culture)
to   our relationship
by telling   you
    "my foots hurt"
but
    you cancelled it
by correcting my grammar
(so you thought)
by saying   "feet"

BRING ME YOUR LOVE

POWERFUL WORDS OF LOVE
by Beverly A. Russell

I used to sit and think:
how could I help
         my beautiful Black people?
how could I uplift my people
and   make this a better world?

I had no money   but
         I wanted to do something
         for us.
(I did not want to be a martyr
         for the ignorance of this world.)

Over the years
         it dawned on me
I could best inspire Black people
with   words of courage and wisdom
--   powerful words of love.

PART THREE: WE BE QUEENS

WE BE QUEENS
(for Ma Rainey, Bessie Smith, Billie Holiday, Alberta Hunter, Betty Carter, Leontyne Price, Marian Anderson, Josephine Baker, and other soulful Black sisters)
by Beverly A. Russell

We be queens
We be Egyptian queens
We be Ethiopian queens
We be ancient/earth queens

Yeah, we be queens

We be blues queens
We be jazz queens
We be soul queens

Yeah, we be queens

We be ancient African queens

POEM FOR REVOLUTIONARY WOMEN
(for Winnie Mandela and Coretta Scott King)
by Hazel Clayton Harrison

The river is wide and the river is deep
    but   i got promises to keep
i'm tired but it don't matter none
they killed my man and jailed my son
but the son keeps risin' each morning
and i gotta get up
'cause a woman's work is never done
    from early morn to setting sun
    from early morn to setting sun

SECRETS OF A BLACK WOMAN
by Uilani Enola Jackmon

I walk tall
so they will wonder
    why
        I am confident

I laugh loud
so they will wonder
    what amuses me

I talk little
so they will wonder
    what
    I am thinking

I walk tall
I laugh loud
I talk little
    so
they will always wonder
    but
will they ever know?

AN UNCOMMON, COMMON WOMAN
by Leon Knight

Mother Rosa Parks,
you were   so right
             so fitting,
             so appropriate:
a seamstress
        a common job,
        nothing to look up to
        but (now we know)
        nothing to look down on --
        (and Jesus was a carpenter
        who washed other men's feet)
riding a bus --
        not a fancy car
        but a public bus --
sitting after a long day's work --
        tired
        (I know the feeling well)
        wanting to get home
        and take your shoes off.
Then came your call:
by claiming your right
        to sit
you taught us
        to stand   up.
By your saying "no" to them,
we learned to say "yes"
        for overselves

An uncommon, common woman,
Mother Rosa, you were so right
        for us.

WE BE QUEENS

MAMA'S HANDS
by Pauline Bady

Mama's hands
are gentle hands
they are firm hands
with loving touches that
      hold me
        squeeze me
        caress me.

Mama's hands
are hands that work hard
and sometimes blister
they are hands that
are sometimes tired
and need rest.

Mama's hands
are peaceful hands
in times of prayer
      they are waving hands
      they are caring hands
      they are gentle hands
      they are firm hands

Mama's hands are
      loving hands. . .

WOMEN RAISE MENS
by Angela Kinamore

Though I been treated
    as second class
since put upon this earth
and told I can't do
    without men,
they forget one thing --
    women raise mens!
I know mens thoughts
    before they think them
I know mens better
    than they know themselves
I know how to get along
without mens   (if I have to)

I've carried mens in my womb
I've made life pleasant for mens
    giving my love and wisdom
    teaching mens how to survive
    soaring mens sights
        to higher heights

I do all right raising mens
    in a fatherless world
    teaching mens to grow strong
    to learn how to carry on . . .
Women keep the race going
    the bloodline flowing
perfecting each diamond
of a child . . . sho nuff'
To be a woman is great
    for I am a queen
    in my own way
Mens should reflect on that,
open their eyes and   see
just how great women can be
'cause   we raise mens!

THE NILE FLOWS NORTH
by Linda Benner-Parker

I have heard African drums
    beating out warnings
of slave-traders on our shores.
I have heard the cries
of   Black men,
       Black women,
       Black children
kidnapped from our homeland
hundreds of years before.

(why   do i hear each tear?)

AGING LADY OF LOVE
by Maryetta Kelsick Boose

Aging lady
    hanging on a corner
    looking for a john,
how did the fine furs
    the fancy clothes
    the good things in life
your pimp promised
    escape you
so that you find yourself,
    an aging lady of love,
working corners
    alone?

SONG OF A SINGLE MOTHER
by Lorraine Bryant

I am talented, beautiful, and black
    with so very much to give,
    with so very much to offer
And I love the life I live.

Any song I could sing, I sang it
Any book I could read, I read.
But they told me I wasn't worth it,
    and this messed with my head.
They told me I couldn't make it,
but that's something I didn't know.
Still, at times my confidence left me
    and my head I would carry low.

My self esteem was eventually lost,
my guts eventually spilled.
But even when I was down, way down,
I never gave up the will --
    the will to be somebody,
    the very best I can be.
And that very will inside me
    led to my destiny.

Now I am strong, renewed and ready
to make my dreams come true
And when they say bad things about me,
I say, "Who's listening to you?"

For it's not the school I attended
nor the color of my skin.
What makes me the woman I am
is the "will" I carry within.

WE BE QUEENS

THE "STUFF" OF HEROES
(for Mari)
by Ginny Knight

she is not the "stuff" of heroes
not as taught in our history books
and newspapers will not record her efforts

but she was determined
    to have the best possible chance
        for her child
    no matter how difficult
        it proved to be
            for her

and she struggled
    struggled alone
        to provide food
        and a stable home
    no matter how tired
        she often felt
and she endured
    the long days
        and the lonely nights

hers is a lucky child
    a dandilion-blowing
    cloud-dreaming child
a child whose jeans are
    patched with love
        and smell of sunshine
a rope-jumping, hide-and-seek playing
    child

a lucky child
    seen safely to school
        prepared for life
with love and education

she is not the "stuff" of heroes
you will not find her name in the history books

NIGHT SONG
by Shirley Dougan King

Much has been said about Black Mammy
but little about
                  Black Mother
You remember her -- the slave woman
who had to stand   silent
as she watched her children
being sold away   (silent)
as one would do with a litter of pups;
       the one who gave
her life-milk to little "master"
while her child cried hungry and alone;
       the one who knew
freedom came too late for her
but   washed Miss Lucy's clothes
just so hers could buy those books
       for learning;
the one who watched her man hanging
from   that tree of sorrow
yet   (in the face of master)
       strong for her children

Black Mother --
The one who hates the hell hole
       she's living in,
but   scrubbing her children
every Sunday for that bit of heaven
       Sunday morning services.

Black Mother,
You remember her --
       the one who got all joy
       and pride from your successes,
The one who wore that old coat
so you could have a new one;
       the one who taught you
what love - unselfish really meant;
       the one who volumes
       could be written about.

DO ME A FAVOR
by Diane E. Sterling

I have heard enough
of   "Sweet Brown Sugar"
Don't call me that
    anymore
I am sugar-free

I have heard too often
    "Hey, Mama"
and I get way-too tired
of always turning around:
she's never there
my mama (your mama)

Please don't holler "Baby"
'cuz my children are grown
and you scare me,
    make me wonder
      if I'm through
nurturing seeds
    alone.

After all these years,
now that we've both grown old
    do me a favor --
call me by my name
    'cuz I like it
Then   leave me alone.

PART FOUR: OUR CHILDREN WILL INHERIT

OUR CHILDREN WILL INHERIT
by Ginny Knight

*"our children will inherit
what we give them...."*
(from a Yoruba praise song)

the pattern is set
trimmed too close
to allow for alterations

it could be changed
      by hard work
and   clever patching

if anyone is interested
and dedicated enough
    to do it.

PRAYER FOR A BLACK CHILD
by Mary J. Kyle

Her sadness hones my blunted edge of pain
That one, like hers, cut swiftly to the heart
Of self-diminished, struggling to regain
Some shred of pride race-hatred ripped apart.
The unexpected slur -- flung by her peers
Who learn, too young, to snicker and degrade
The victim of their scorn -- spawns tears
To cleanse the gaping wound of trust betrayed
    She is so small, so vulnerable, dear Lord,
To senseless jeers; give her an open mind,
Let aching ease, become a minor chord
Within the symphony of humankind.
      Awaken Soul, the secret place inside
      That lights our fire for a cause-denied.

TWO IN ONE
by Odessa Cleveland

I am Africa's rhythm
I am American's glory.
Red river
White river
Yellowstone river
Green river
Congo river glides
through my veins
Me?
In a melting pot?
Oh, no!
I am cultural pluralism
Two in one -
You got that!

BLIND CONSCIENCE
by Patricia M. Johnson

Dark eyes smolder
in ashes of life:

Oh, child
you sit in the rubble
of our good intentions --
bloated belly,
a target for pain,
flies drawing nourishment
from your wretched tears,
body eroding in desert heat.

Our fat grain bins
await prices to exceed
costs of production,
while ghetto rats gnaw
at blankets of security
and African children drown
in a dry sea of hunger.

OUR CHILDREN WILL INHERIT

LULLABYE TO A SWEET BROWN BABY
by Alcleata Hamilton Williams

Rock-a-bye sweet brown baby
Close your eyes and sleep
Dream this dream, sweet brown baby
Where your roots lie deep

La la la sweet brown baby
Sail down the mighty Benue
Child of the Kingdom of Ghana and Mali
Product of Timbuktu

Can you hear the Tribal Griot?
Feel the talking drum?
Smell the spicy peanut stew
Taste the steamy fou fou?

Rock-a-bye sweet brown baby
While I tell you as you coo
You're part of a glorious past
The American future too.

POSITIVE REFLECTIONS
by Hasani B. Julian

Me and Keesha
walk straight in
Mama's and Daddy's
shadow, 'cause
if we step out
of the lines,
we make a monster.

RUNNING, RUNNING, RUNNING
by Rosa Bogar

Black child, running
    wild
        running wild
        black child

You are only half grown
You can't make it
    on your own
running, running
wild   black child

It seems you're seeing life
    through one eye
        don't know if to laugh
        or cry

Running running running
wild   black child

OUR CHILDREN WILL INHERIT

WIND CHIMES (For JoAnn)
by Sandy Macebuh

Wind chimes   made like a rainbow,
    hang in the window,
tinkling back to a long-ago
rainbow-poem   I wrote for a girl.
She searched the sky for something
bright.   She looked for
    the pot of gold.
Now she haunts me, staring blankly
from the page of an empty book
    with a rainbow
in the corner of its blue-satin cover.
The satin of her coffin haunts me.

Her young life departed the city
where rainbows don't show themselves
between tall buildings
and all the impoverished places.
    In the place of bright dreams,
she was offered   wind chimes
    to brighten the ghetto,
rainbow patches to sew over torn clothing,
rainbow lapel pins - all the tin rainbows.
When she suffered discrimination,
the dope she took offered
    better hallucinations,
still   brighter   rainbows.
She haunts me   (not as a pale ghost)
in rainbows,   in a smoke
    of Blackness
She haunts me   in color
as she haunts the world
with its gothic horror of the poor,
    the creepy dark buildings,
and   all the warehouses of souls.
Mostly, she haunts me
    with her cries
that turn wind chimes   wild.

ON THE WINGS OF THEIR HOPES
by Hazel Bell

I move easily over paths made smooth
      by my ancestors
Warm in the glow
of their achievements
      I rest for a spell
In the night, their expectations
      light my way
Soaring high   on the wings
of their hopes
I see places they could only dream of
Perhaps   my children will live there.

SING CHILDREN SING
by Odessa Cleveland

Our children
      a gift to America
born   under the sign
of red, white, and blue
    flower buds   sprouting
      yearning
they take the spirit of life
    forward   forward
      to become adults --
their songs   an anthem
      of America
Sing,   children, sing!

PART FIVE: MAKE STRONG MEN SING

MOTHER DIDN'T TELL ME TO CRY
(but to fight back)
by Gene A. Williams

Mother didn't tell me to cry
      no, never
She didn't tell me to sit back
and pout about nothing,
to sit in the back of the bus
      and think about "them" and "us"

She didn't tell me to cry
      but to fight back
with words --
      To burn some midnight oil,
      Carry my books all the way home;
      To study some math
      and chemistry and all the earth,
      biological and physical sciences
      history and humane letters.

She told me to read the "psalms"
of   James Baldwin,
Ralph Ellison, and Richard Wright
      to study all the wrongs
      that parade as rights

To make sense of "Daylight Saving Time"
and "Monk Time," "Coltrane Time"
      and all the "Bad Times"
      that make strong men sing.

Mother didn't tell me to cry
      but to fight back
with   weapons of peace
      the words of war,
      the songs
      that savor the meanings
      and moods
      and an ancient solitude.

FOR THE MEN WHO SIRE US
(as evidence of your behavior)
by Phyllis J. Sloan

Look into our eyes
so you may know your own.

I am Sha-De of North Carolina
    my mother was your slave mistress
    my hair is brown-wavy
    my skin is cream
    we   my mother and me
were your property

I am Kim Lee of Vietnam
    you never married my mother
(your wife back home wouldn't let you)
    my country calls me "half-breed"
    I am a stranger here

I am Billy of the projects
      I am your love child
        (my mother's love for you)
everybody says we look alike
      you and me
but   I don't know that

We are burdened by knowing
    who sired us
without knowing any father
Look into our eyes
    so you may see
        your own.

THE CROSSING
by Leon Knight

I don't understand
    why
so many of us survived

when we crossed the bloody ocean
    in come stinking hold:
when we crossed the Mississippi
    shouting "jubilee";
when we crossed the Mason-Dixon
    'cause we heard Detroit was free;
when we crossed the high Sierras
    seeing California gold

But we are survivors
    --tough, courageous dreamers
    --hard-muscled, strong-boned

So why do I find it so difficult
    to cross this street
    and go home?

MAN ON THE CORNER
by Sharon C. Terry

Sitting down, talking trash
    wasting time,
telling jokes, pitching pennies,
    drinking wine --
    Don't you think its time
    to get an education,
    to find a job (or two),
    make your family proud
    of you?

Man on the corner.

dropping pills, pushing junk,
    taking pretense-thrills
faking courage, flashing green,
    yet ducking bills --
    Don't you think its time
    to stop feeling inferior,
    to look people in the eye,
    to hold your head up high?

Man on the corner.

MAKE STRONG MEN SING

DE WATERS AND DE CRIES
by Kenya Keita Kenyatta Samuels

de waters are as cool as de midnight breeze
as beautiful as de stilling sunset
as precious as de lord our God
as fun as your first love
as quiet and calm as de softly calling loon
as easy going as canoeing

oh our softly calling waters,
who hears the desperate cries
of de sad, sick, black man
    why should he suffer so?

Oh can't de lords of de waters help?
    I cry to you
let me hear de desperate cries,
let me suffer de hurt and doubts
let me help, oh blessed beautiful waters,
hear my cry as I hear yours
Oh de beautiful, calm, wonderful
    stillness of de waters.

FATHER TO SON
by Sidney Singleton Sr.

Some men search
   for riches or treasures
while others search
   for hidden pleasures.
Some derive satisfaction
   from fortune and fame
while others get thrills
   from dangerous games.
But after all is said and done
it's a joyous feeling
   to share time
      with a son.

THE GUITAR MAN
by George D. Clabon

hey Maurice
   man
you sho' could play
   that rhythm
when we were in
   the cro-shades

going in circles had 'em
   screaming
women crying out
   mo', mo'

couldn't read no music
   never had
taught by your uncle
   chuck b
and the band said
   play on
play on
   guitar man

PART SIX: SOMETHING HAS AROUSED ME

SOMETHING HAS AROUSED ME
by Beverly A. Russell

Something has aroused me
stirring me
making me more alive
more aware
glad to be alive
it's a feeling you get
when you remember
I mean remember way back
like before you were born
like when you remember
your ancestors
and that they came from Africa
and that makes you a part of Africa
and you feel so glad
that you are black and alive
and it feels so good
    remembering

THE BLACK PRESS
by Arlee Bullard Blakey

As I read the daily papers
    about crimes and such
I do not see in there
    the good Blacks do, very much.

Pictures of Blacks in jail are there,
    or who rob and steal.
But it's just the opposite
    how the Black media feels.

Books by Johnson Publishing
    or by Guild Press
Tell it like it is -- the yearnings
    and the black mass's success.

I was not aware of all the things
    Black folks really did.
Reading those publications showed
    what the daily papers hid

Why should we be ignorant
    when there's the Black press
focusing on issues, interests,
    courageous acts and our progress?

Subscribing to these publications
    is just one endeavor,
but by giving them support
the Black press will be around forever

SOMETHING HAS AROUSED ME

SATURDAY AT THE INGLEWOOD FARMERS' MARKET
by Hazel Clayton Harrison

*"Potatoes   Tomatoes
     Green beans
Apples   Oranges
     Collard greens"*

Early on Saturday morning
     before the sun comes up
     a farmer starts unloadin' his truck
     Police stand guard
     at the street barricade
     while street vendors sell
     fresh-squeezed lemonade

Look there's a square dance
     in the middle of the street
     the ladies swirl and move their feet
     senior citizens are doin' the do-si-do
     "Swing yo' partner to and fro."
     The smell of popcorn/candy fill the air
     It's better than bein' at the county fair.

*"Potatoes   Tomatoes
     Green beans
Apples   Oranges
     Collard greens"*

HOSPITALITY IN LA
(by a Minnesota visitor)
by Phyllis J. Sloan

surrounded by ocean sounds
energized by the power of the Pacific
    our Sunday morning beach walk
we laid back
encircled by loving portraits of a year ago
    their eyes smiled: full of each other
their daughters played Monopoly with mine
(as good, fun loving girls still do)
he shared photographs of their travels
    sunsets/mountains/waterfalls
while the scent of slow barbeque
serenaded -- yes serenaded all our thoughts
in the kitchen --finely manicured hands
    fixed creamed corn
--the hard way -- off the cob and spiced
    (like my grandma used to)
she said it was her mother's recipe

L.A. is 2,000 miles away
but   really
        not so far.

SOMETHING HAS AROUSED ME

IF YOU DON'T KNOW
by Dennis DeLoach

Once I had a bad meal
and up I was shook
entertained by a woman
who didn't know how to cook.

Said she wanted to please me
no matter what it took
I said it would please me better
if she learned how to cook.

I don't get too excited
about how a woman looks
if she knows nothing
about a recipe book.

If she's got bad legs,
that I can overlook --
I'll carry her to the kitchen
if she's going there to cook

Take me like a fish,
put me on your hook
But you can throw me back
if you don't know how to cook

THE BIG HOUSE ON THE HILL
by Hazel Clayton Harrison

My momma was a housekeeper
my daddy worked in the mill.
They worked from sun up to sun down
but we never got a house on the hill.

Those houses on the hill
were so big and white,
while we lived in a three-room shack
without electric light.

Not long ago, my momma passed away,
but I'll always hear her say,
"Don't you cry, Son, 'cause it's God's will,
I'm finally gonna live in that big house on the hill."

IMMORTAL AFRIKAN SPIRIT
(an excerpt from)
by Jamal Ali

Like the lion
my family is my pride
to ancient Afrikan spirits
ancestral to my own
I am a living monument
      instead
      of chiseled stone
my spiritual lineage
fires the night darkness
shining deep inside
it is the source
of my inner force
a sign of the Divine
that translates, in my mind
as   Afrika

SOMETHING HAS AROUSED ME

STRONG BLACK WOMAN
by Phyllis J. Sloan

molded into being
    a strong black woman
so strong   (never thought
    i'd be this strong)
pottery   clay
baked in the kiln   of life
    experience upon experience
thrown into the hottest fire
fired   into   being
pottery -- a strong black woman.

AIN'T NEVER GONNA DIE
by Charlene Higginbotham

gonna rhyme my heart
    to the beat of all that's livin',

ain't never gonna die,
ain't never gonna die.

gonna laugh and shout
    for all that God has given,

ain't never gonna cry,
ain't never gonna cry.

gonna carry my people
    through the dream that Martin gave them.
gonna lift them up
    with the love that's in the rhythm

ain't never gonna die,
ain't never gonna die.

OUR BLACK PROTECTORS
(Sao Mateus, Brazil)
by Antonia Apolinario

     The Congada:
the drums echoing sounds of Africa
in assimilated Afro-Catholic festivities
-- sounds of my infancy in Sao Mateus.
Small, old white-houses,
freshly waxed floors,
     colonial churches to honor
Sau Mateus and Sau Benedito
--our black protectors.

Women in cotton white-dresses
and headdresses
contrasted against their smooth, blackest skins
     moved in sisterhood with Mary
in devotion and suffering;
going to Mass
In the church,   the incense in the air,
the rush of rosary beads,
the cool holy-water
     sprinkled to bless us all
     angels and cherubs
in their pinkest color and bluest eyes
watching us from the gold altars.
The smell of wax from candles
burned in thanksgiving for graces obtained.
     Altar boys and priests
in starched, white-blue robes.
The ritual carried in Latin --
a mysterious language
for a six-year-old   "Amen!"

Outside, the feira (street market)
     is alive again --
re-encounter with friends
who labored all week in the farms
to bring their fruits to town --
     fresh catfish, fragrant "coentro"
     golden precious squash.
Sturdy homes   and people
of this river town halfway
to Salvador, Bahia

SOMETHING HAS AROUSED ME

WHAT'S DESTINED TO COME
(for Winnie and Nelson)
by Angela Kinamore

Winnie Mandela,
a constant reminder
    of one's inner strength
    of the power to endure
    any test to pay
    the price of freedom
        for our people,
forever holding on to the vision
of   what's destined to come.

Nelson Mandela,
a mightly spirit,
     a great warrior
who   will   one day
              be free
and manifest his dreams
hidden deep   in the soul
of   what's destined to come.

Winnie and Nelson,
know that we pray with you
and think of you every day.

We also hold strong
    to the vision
    of a great Anzania,
    the new world
that's destined to come.

Then we can all return
(spiritually)   home to Africa,
        the Motherland
        that we love
to begin (again)....
    what's destined to come.

BEARERS OF BLACKNESS

NOTES ABOUT THE AUTHORS

JAMAL ALI is an engineer and freelance writer.
ANTONIA APOLINARIO was born in Sao Mateus, Brazil and currently lives in Minneapolis.
PAULINE BADY lives in Los Angeles.
HAZEL BELL dedicates these poems to her family.
LINDA BENNER-PARKER lives in Sacramento, California.
ARLEE BULLARD BLAKEY is a musical composer and writer.
ROSA BOGAR is the author of *Black Woman Sorrow*.
MARYETTA KELSICK BOOSE lives in California.
MAURICE W. BRITTS is the author of *Billy Williams, Minnesota's Assistant Governor*.
LORRAINE BRYANT is a single parent who lives in Minnesota.
ALBERTO O. CAPPAS was born in Yauco, Puerto Rico and now lives in New York.
LOUIS A. CHASE lives in Los Angeles.
GEORGE D. CLABON has had poems published in *On Being Black*, *Do Black Men Cry*, and *The Butterfly Tree*.
ODESSA CLEVELAND lives in Hollywood, California.
DENNIS DELOACH is the publisher of *Heritage* magazine.
BERNARD V. FINNEY Jr. is a library consultant in New York.
HAZEL CLAYTON HARRISON is co-author of *A Most Defiant Act* and editor of *On Being Black*.
CHARLENE HIGGINBOTHAM graduated from Michigan State University and lives in Minnesota.
UILANI ENOLA JACKMON was born in Honolulu and now lives in St. Paul, Minnesota.
PATRICIA M. JOHNSON is editor of *The Moccasin, The Turning Wheel*, and *Prairie Bread*.
HASANI B. JULIAN is a librarian with the Oakland Public Library System.
ESSIE CALDWELL KAMMIN is a poet who aspires to become a fiction writer and playwright.
ANGELA KINAMORE is the poetry editor of Essence magazine.
SHIRLEY DOUGAN KING is a teacher in the Minneapolis Public Schools.

BEARERS OF BLACKNESS

GINNY KNIGHT is an artist and co-author of *A Most Defiant Act*.

LEON KNIGHT is author of *Some Words Have Wings* and *Vera's Return*.

MARY J. KYLE is a free-lance writer and a published author. She is currently working on a book.

SANDY MACEBUH lives in Orange, California.

BEVERLY A. RUSSELL was born in Riverside, California and currently lives in Hollywood.

KENYA KEITA KENYATTA SAMUELS is in the 8th grade at Nicollet Junior High School in Minnesota.

SIDNEY SINGLETON SR. was born in Louisiana and now lives in Los Angeles.

PHYLLIS J. SLOAN is editor of *Full Circle Six*.

DIANE E. STERLING works for the Minneapolis Civil Rights Department.

SHARON C. TERRY is a native Californian and is proud to have her work published in *Bearers of Blackness*.

KEN WIBECAN lives in Southern California and writes a weekly editorial column and a weekly jazz column for the *Long Beach Press-Telegram*.

ALCLEATA HAMILTON WILLIAMS is an artist as well as a poet, who lives in Los Angeles.

CYNTHIA WILLIAMS was born and bred in Minnesota.

GENE A. WILLIAMS is a poet of the 80s with roots in the 60s. He teaches school in Los Angeles.